Color-Changing Animals

by Valerie Yaw

Consultant: Hopi E. Hoekstra
Associate Professor, Department of Organismic & Evolutionary Biology
Curator of Mammals, Museum of Comparative Zoology
Harvard University

BEARPORT
PUBLISHING

New York, New York

Credits

Cover and Title Page, © fivespots/Shutterstock; 4L, © Christian Musat/Shutterstock; 4R, © John Van Decker/Alamy; 5T, © McPhoto/blickwinkel/Alamy; 5B, © Liew Weng Keong/Shutterstock; 6L, © Dwight Kuhn/Dwight Kuhn Photography; 6R, © Joel Johndro/iStockphoto; 7, © Photolibrary/SuperStock; 8, © Joe Austin Photography/Alamy; 9, © Tom & Pat Leeson/Ardea; 10L, © Thomas Reavill/Alamy; 10R, © Jane Gould/Alamy; 11, © Imagebroker/SuperStock; 12, © Stubblefield Photography/Shutterstock; 12–13, © Roger Steene/Image Quest Marine; 13, © Fred Bavendam/Minden Pictures; 14, © Lynette Schimming; 15, © CLChang/Shutterstock; 16–17, © Dwight Kuhn/Dwight Kuhn Photography; 17, © Wolfgang Kaehler/Corbis; 18T, © Kike Calvo/Visual & Written/Alamy; 18B, © Mark Conlin/Visual & Written/SuperStock; 19, © WaterFrame/Alamy; 20, © Gigerichová Lydie/Isifa Image Service/Alamy; 21, © Sue Robinson/Shutterstock; 22T, © All Canada Photos/SuperStock; 22M, © WaterFrame/Alamy; 22B, © Philipp Gilli/Shutterstock; 23, © Taboga/Shutterstock.

Publisher: Kenn Goin
Editorial Director: Adam Siegel
Creative Director: Spencer Brinker
Design: Dawn Beard Creative
Cover: Kim Jones
Photo Researcher: Picture Perfect Professionals, LLC

Library of Congress Cataloging-in-Publication Data

Yaw, Valerie.
  Color-changing animals / by Valerie Yaw.
      p. cm. — (Animals with super powers)
  Includes bibliographical references and index.
  ISBN-13: 978-1-61772-122-9 (library binding)
  ISBN-10: 1-61772-122-0 (library binding)
  1. Animal defenses—Juvenile literature. 2. Animal communication—Juvenile literature.
  3. Camouflage (Biology)—Juvenile literature. I. Title.
  QL759.Y39 2011
  591.47'2—dc22

                          2010038283

For more information, write to Bearport Publishing Company, Inc., 101 Fifth Avenue, Suite 6R, New York, New York 10003. Printed in the United States of America in North Mankato, Minnesota.

122010
10810CGD

10 9 8 7 6 5 4 3 2 1

Contents

Quick-Change Artists

Imagine having the power to transform your appearance. Certain animals can change the color of their skin or fur to match different colors in their **habitats**. This special form of **camouflage** helps them disappear into their surroundings. Hidden from sight, they can stay safe from hungry **predators**—or sneak up on their **prey** unnoticed.

Seahorse

Goldenrod
crab spider

4

Staying hidden isn't the only thing animals can do with their color-changing abilities. Some creatures can display bright colors to share information with other animals, attract a **mate**, or startle and confuse an enemy.

In this book, you'll meet eight of these quick-change artists. Among them are an octopus that transforms its color and shape to look like other animals, a **lizard** that uses bright colors and patterns to **communicate**, and a fish that changes its color as often as it changes its mood.

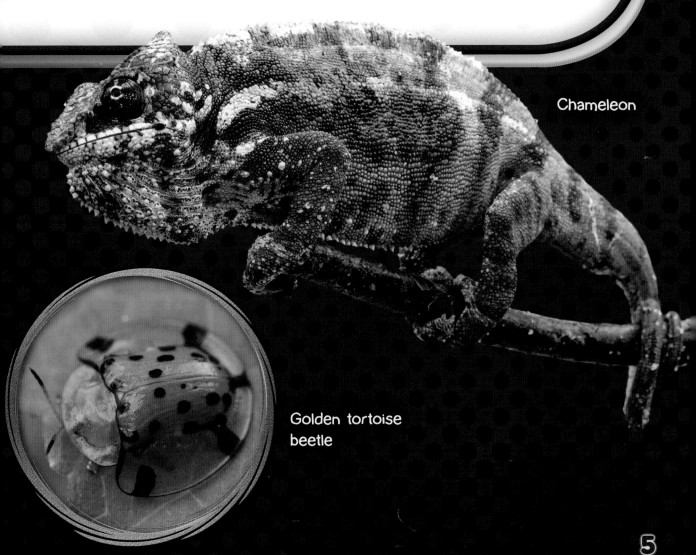

Chameleon

Golden tortoise beetle

Gray Tree Frog

Gray tree frogs aren't always gray. They can change the color of their skin to shades of green, brown, or almost black. How do they do it? Gray tree frogs have special color **cells**, called **chromatophores**, in their skin. When different chromatophores get bigger or smaller, the frog's skin changes color.

The ability to change color helps gray tree frogs blend in with bark, **moss**, and leaves in their **environment**—which helps them stay safe. Once the frogs have changed color, it is no longer easy for predators, such as birds, snakes, and skunks, to find and eat them.

Gray tree frogs live in parts of the United States and Canada. They spend much of their adult lives in trees.

The gray tree frog's bumpy skin also helps it stay hidden. Its texture matches the rough surface of tree bark.

Other kinds of frogs can change their colors. However, most can't change to as many different colors as the gray tree frog.

Snowshoe Hare

Fierce killers such as coyotes, wolves, and foxes hunt the snowshoe hare. How does this small animal stay safe from these dangerous predators? One way is to make a speedy escape. The snowshoe hare can run up to 27 miles per hour (43 kph). An even better way to avoid danger, though, is to stay out of sight!

The snowshoe hare lives in the forests of Canada and the northern United States. During the summer, its fur is brown and gray, allowing it to blend in with twigs and bushes on the forest floor. In the fall, the snowshoe hare begins to grow a thick, fluffy white **coat** that will match the snow-covered ground and trees in winter. When the snow melts in the spring, the hare **sheds** its white fur and grows a brown coat again. Changing its fur color in spring and fall helps keep the snowshoe hare hidden all year.

It takes about ten weeks for a snowshoe hare's coat color to change.

The snowshoe hare got its name from its large back feet. They help the hare move across the snow without sinking in— just like snowshoes.

The snowshoe hare's thick white coat helps keep it warm through the winter.

9

Cuttlefish

The cuttlefish can change the color and pattern of its skin in less than a second—faster than any other animal! Whether it's swimming near dull-colored rocks and sand or a brightly colored **coral reef**, it can instantly match its environment. This camouflage helps the cuttlefish hide from predators, including sharks, other large fish, dolphins, and seals.

The cuttlefish also uses its camouflage to sneak up and attack animals such as fish and crabs. However, if its prey does spot it, the cuttlefish has another **strategy** ready. It creates dazzling waves of color on its skin to **mesmerize** its prey. When the animal stops to watch the flashing colors, it's an easy target for the hungry cuttlefish.

There are more than 100 kinds of cuttlefish. They live in warm oceans near Africa, Asia, Australia, and Europe.

Despite their name, cuttlefish aren't fish. They're **mollusks**, a group of animals that includes slugs, octopuses, snails, clams, and squids.

The flamboyant cuttlefish is poisonous. When threatened, it creates a warning display of bright colors and puffed-up arms to tell its enemy that it is dangerous.

Mimic Octopus

All octopuses can change their colors, but the **mimic** octopus has an extra-special way of keeping predators from attacking. The eight-armed creature can change its color and shape to disguise itself as another kind of animal! For example, if a damselfish is about to attack, the octopus can make itself look like one of the damselfish's predators—a banded sea snake. To do so, the mimic octopus **imitates** the wide stripes of color on a sea snake's body. It also covers up six of its arms with sand and then spreads out its other two. The octopus then looks so much like a sea snake that the damselfish is fooled into leaving it alone.

True masters of disguise, mimic octopuses can imitate the colors and shapes of up to 13 different animals.

Surprisingly, cuttlefish and octopuses are color blind. How, then, do they match the colors in their environments so closely? Scientists are still investigating this mystery. Part of the answer may lie in a certain kind of chromatophore in their skin that reflects the colors of their surroundings.

mimic octopus disguised as a banded sea snake

Mimic octopuses live in tropical seas near Southeast Asia.

banded sea snake

Golden Tortoise Beetle

The golden tortoise beetle usually has a bright, shiny gold shell. However, if a bird, spider, or other enemy comes close, it can make itself appear to be a very different-looking and much less tasty insect—a ladybug! The golden tortoise beetle mimics a ladybug by making its shell clear, revealing the red-orange color and black spots that are just underneath. The beetle's quick color change helps it avoid becoming a meal for a hungry predator.

The golden tortoise beetle lives in North America. It doesn't hunt other animals for food. Instead, it eats the leaves of plants.

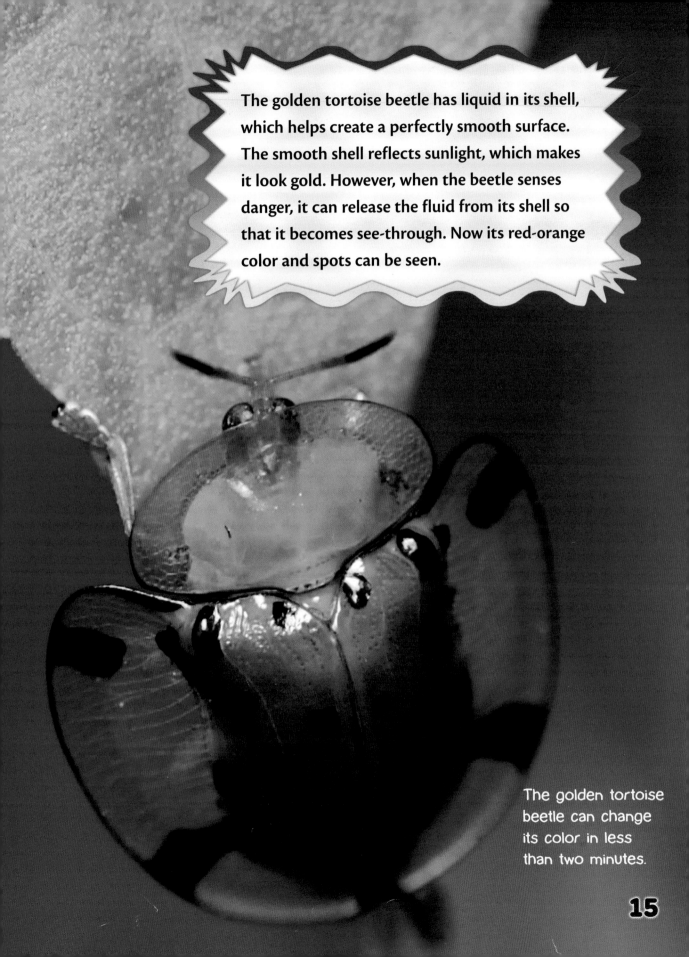

The golden tortoise beetle has liquid in its shell, which helps create a perfectly smooth surface. The smooth shell reflects sunlight, which makes it look gold. However, when the beetle senses danger, it can release the fluid from its shell so that it becomes see-through. Now its red-orange color and spots can be seen.

The golden tortoise beetle can change its color in less than two minutes.

Chameleon

There are more than 150 **species** of chameleons, but only some of them have the ability to change their colors. Each of these species has its own range of colors and patterns that it can display. Some of these lizards change only from brown to green, but others can turn pink, turquoise, orange, red, yellow, or purple!

Certain kinds of chameleons change color to blend in with their environment. However, the lizards usually change their color to be noticed. The main reason they display such eye-catching colors is to send messages to other chameleons. They can flash different colors and patterns to signal that they're looking for a mate or ready to defend their **territory**.

It takes as little as 20 seconds for some chameleons to change the colors and patterns of their skin.

Chameleons live in Africa, the Middle East, India, Sri Lanka, and parts of Europe. Almost half of the world's species live in Madagascar, an island off the southeastern coast of Africa.

Like many other color-changing animals, chameleons change the size of the chromatophores, or special color cells, in their skin to alter their appearance.

Seahorse

The seahorse is an odd-looking fish. It has a horse-like head and a monkey-like tail. Males also have a kangaroo-like pouch. Some kinds of seahorses have another special quality—the power to change color using chromatophores in their skin.

A seahorse's usual color helps it hide from predators such as crabs and large fish. Its camouflage is so good that it's almost impossible to find among clumps of sea grass or clusters of coral. However, seahorses sometimes change their color based on their mood. Whether they're excited or scared, they can use color to show how they feel.

The colors seahorses can display vary by species. Different kinds of seahorses can become red, pink, orange, yellow, blue, green, white, brown, or black. They can also show patterns, such as stripes or spots.

Seahorses live in warm, shallow ocean water, near coral reefs, sea grass beds, or mangrove trees.

A pair of male and female seahorses will change color when they greet each other every day and when they mate.

Goldenrod Crab Spider

The goldenrod crab spider can change its color from white to yellow by producing a yellow liquid in its body. It can change back to white by releasing the liquid from its body. For a long time, scientists thought the goldenrod crab spider changed its color so that it could sit unnoticed on a white or yellow flower while it hunted. When a bee or other insect visited the flower, the hidden spider could **ambush** it.

However, recent studies have shown that the spider's color change may not help it catch prey after all. Does the color change help the spider in another way? Scientists aren't sure. They are still studying this creature to discover more about how its amazing ability to change color helps it survive.

The goldenrod crab spider spends most of its time on flowers such as daisies, sunflowers, and goldenrods in North America and Europe.

It takes a goldenrod crab spider between 10 and 25 days to turn from white to yellow. The reverse change takes only 5 or 6 days.

Only adult female goldenrod crab spiders can change color.

More About
Color-Changing Animals

orange patches

Gray tree frog

The gray tree frog has bright orange or yellow patches on the undersides of its back legs. When the frog jumps, a predator might see the bright color and get startled—giving the frog extra time to escape.

If the mimic octopus's disguises don't fool its predators, it has another way of defending itself. It can squirt a cloud of dark ink that may distract its predator and make the octopus harder to see. The mimic octopus can then make a fast getaway.

Seahorses can grow hard knobs or threads of skin on their bodies to help them hide among bumpy coral or strands of seaweed. Sometimes, tiny plant-like organisms called algae grow on the seahorses and help them blend into their environment even more.

Cuttlefish don't just use their colors to hide. They also use them to communicate with each other. During breeding season, male cuttlefish produce striking displays of color to attract females and tell other males to stay away.

Seahorses

Cuttlefish

Glossary

ambush (AM-bush) to attack from a hidden position

camouflage (KAM-uh-flahzh) colors and markings on an animal's body that help it blend in with its surroundings

cells (SELZ) the basic, microscopic parts of an animal or plant

chromatophores (kroh-MAT-uh-forz) cells that contain color or reflect light

coat (KOHT) an animal's fur

communicate (kuh-MYOO-nuh-kayt) to share information

coral reef (KOR-uhl REEF) a group of rock-like structures formed from the skeletons of sea animals called coral polyps; usually found in shallow tropical waters

environment (en-VYE-ruhn-muhnt) the area where an animal or plant lives, and all the things, such as weather, that affect that place

habitats (HAB-uh-tats) places in nature where animals or plants normally live

imitates (IM-uh-tayts) copies

lizard (LIZ-urd) a type of reptile with a scaly body and tail; it is closely related to snakes

mate (MAYT) one of a pair of animals that have young together

mesmerize (MEZ-muh-ryez) to fascinate

mimic (MIM-ik) to copy

mollusks (MOL-uhsks) animals with no spine and a soft body, usually protected by a hard shell

moss (MAWSS) a fuzzy green plant that sometimes covers rocks or tree bark

predators (PRED-uh-turz) animals that hunt other animals for food

prey (PRAY) animals that are hunted and eaten by other animals

sheds (SHEDZ) loses its fur

species (SPEE-sheez) groups that animals are divided into according to similar characteristics; members of the same species can have offspring together

strategy (STRAT-uh-jee) an action that produces a particular result

territory (TEHR-uh-tor-ee) an area of land that is defended by an animal or a group of animals

Index

Bibliography

Forbes, Peter. *Dazzled and Deceived: Mimicry and Camouflage.* New Haven, CT: Yale University Press (2009).

Hansford, Dave. "Cuttlefish Change Color, Shape-Shift to Elude Predators." *National Geographic News.* August 6, 2008. (news.nationalgeographic.com/news/2008/08/080608-cuttlefish-camouflage-missions.html)

McAlpine, Katherine. "Beetle of Many Colors." *Discover* 28.12 (2007): 16.

O'Day, Kira E. "Conspicuous Chameleons." *PLoS Biology* 6.1 (2008): e21.

Read More

Mitchell, Susan K. *Animals with Crafty Camouflage.* Berkeley Heights, NJ: Enslow (2009).

Schwartz, David M., and Yael Schy. *Where in the Wild? Camouflaged Creatures Concealed . . . and Revealed.* Berkeley, CA: Tricycle Press (2007).

Stewart, Melissa. *How Do Chameleons Change Color?* Tarrytown, NY: Marshall Cavendish (2009).

Learn More Online

To learn more about color-changing animals, visit
www.bearportpublishing.com/AnimalswithSuperPowers

About the Author

Valerie Yaw works for a children's book publisher in New York.
Color-Changing Animals is her first book.